POET'S CREATIVITY WITH A SIDE OF LITERALLY

MILA E. LEESON

To those who have helped me along the way

THE BEGINNING

What is Creative Writing?
What does it even mean,
Young and blind to thy written word,
I wasn't easy for me to see.
I didn't quite get poetry,
Rhymed too much,
It wasn't even analytical and deep,
I preferred short and playful stories,
Yet as I grew and perceived the word under me,
I found my passion,
The passion for simple, playful,
Literary poetry,
Thanks to the people,
I have come to know,
And understand to be,
They helped me start my beginning.

By chance I **ACCIDENTAL** found you, By chance it might **LOVE** have been fate, Oh, but I'm so tired of it being called fate, Fate has left thy heart cracked and cratered, Leaving me in a state of constant disdain, So maybe this isn't fate or destiny, Whatever those damnned prophets say, Maybe these were my choices that led way. Future holds a mystery, Past hold regret, Present holds gifts, gifts I never though I'd get, You were somethig unforetold, Words can't express the love I feel in full, My thoughts twist and turn, But I can't think of those few simple words I thought I always knew what to say, But why do you make my mind go blank, I write for a living so why is this hard, I can hardly describe who you are, But that's a good think, At least that's what eveyone says, There's so much to learn, Is what I've heard.You were my accidental love, Someone who healed a shattered and solemn heart.Now I live for a purpose, A purpose beyond my own, The purpose to live and love from year to year, My heart beats and bleeds only for you my dear.

Little pad floating agasint
the pond, I know I've seen you before,
Likely in a dream maybe in some beyond. Little pad
You trap my gaze, I don't know what to do as you float
away, I reach out my arm streatching as far as it may,
I don't want to fall in the murky water, But I wish you'd just stay.
In another life we are together, I sit upon your pad and dream the day,
away, Yet now I float in the water, Not scared of the murky color.If you go
far, I will follow along, Wether it be under a bridge, Or in a new pond, I
will always follow you into the beyond. My best friend, Never forget me
even when we're further gone, I will always remember our
first little pond, Lilly pad you held me, Held me when were
young, You kept me above the water of my anxious thoughts.
But now I can swim on my own, So go and help others who
can't, Because when I wake up. Dearest Lillian, You'll still
be my best friend.

LILLY PAD

AND

Mom

and dad

don't ever feel

bad. Don't ever feel

bad. Bad for when I cry,

MOM

DAD

Bad for when I sigh. I struggle

to cover my heart. I love you forever

I love you never not. Tears drip down my face

Tears drip down in this ceremonial place. My two

supporting angles, I watch your eyes let me go, I watch

your eyes with happy woes. Mom and Dad, Don't ever feel bad.

Hold me as close as you can, Hold me as you would way back then.

SECOND FAMILY

It wasn't my choice, Thee that I have   come to see,

Are something   dear to me. Something more than

peers, Something more than just friends. These

random people, weird and extraordinary,   Are my

family to   the very end. Even if we all fall apart,

Drift away near or far, These people are my second

home, They all mean the   most of the most

 Second family of my forever home.

I

start as a

seed, Though

there have been seeds

before me, They grow a part

of a tree, Right now, I am Just a

sapling. Soon I will grow my own leaves

Soon I will intertwine

with the grand tree, Then

my roots will become another,

Sprout a new tree that will connect others,

But I will never forget my roots, the tree that

birthed me will always be a part of my little leaves,

Forever a family,
ROOTS

Chaos.

That's all I've

ever seen, Family

full of boys and men,

It's as ironic as one would

think.   Yet,   Here I am,

With a girl from another family, Now

woven into this vast family link, She drips

into thy puddle, It's deeper than you think.

Now she is a part of the chaos, Married to my

brother, But,   A sister-in-law to me,

I welcome her to the madness, As

the pudddle grows,

indefinitely.

DROPLET TO THE SEA

BELOVED DEAD

They lay among the

ground, A contrast to how they never laid

down, These people old, Wise, And true. They didn't

raise me, But I've learned thy tale of the distant   truth,

I wish I would have been there, The period   stories

these tales were formed. Instead I watch the gravestones,

Thinking of what I yet to know, My beloved dead, I wish

to eventually meet your soul. Maybe you know me, You

watch me from the beyond, I hope to know you, when my   body

is long and gone. Beloved dead, wait for me, Until I finally depart.

FILLED

Oh, I hate.

I hate this   place!

I wish to go! I   never

liked it here!   You

wouldn't even   know!

Is what my peers would

hear. I would   exclaim

and preach, This place

is dreadful,   Awful

beyond compare,   Yet

Something keeps   me

going, Something keeps

me sane, My   teachers

there, Dragging   me

from my disdain, Their
will to help,   Their
will to stay,   Keeps
me going until
my last
day

AWFUL PLACE

WITH GRACE

SKIES

IN THE

I salute you as one would   do,

Commander or Chief,   I'm

something more, More than the

ranks you clim, I wish to be with
you, Soaring through the endless
    sky.   Brother so far, I salute
      you so on,

BROTHER

      I
   hope you

come home, I hope you feel my woes

A Pilot you are, Brother

come home, I can't

stand to   see you

all   alone

BROTHER WITH A SHINY BADGE

Siren screech as he

flies down the streets, Stopping crime, But a big brother

on the side, Cool and collected, My brother never

fretted, Badge adorned on his chest, Slevee

cuffs tight on his wrist, And a holster you can't

miss. My brother is a cop. I insist you look it up,

Never miss this man go far, He's always in his cool cop

car, I'll miss him when I'm away, I wish I could stay, My

Brother, I'll miss you always, I'll miss more

and more.

The spotlight falls, There you are, The light follows you, The eyes of

people do to. I watched you perform, I never noticed it before,   I

always thought you   a   bore, I was never   really

sure. You opened   my   eyes, You made   my

heart realize,   You   know how   to

preform, You aren't   little   anymore.

My baby   brother, My

applause   is   for

no   other   They heart

is   adorned,   Even when

I   scorned   but   don't

worry   more,   I'll be with you,

Near and far, Dear   baby   brother.

CURTAIN CALLS

Doggy
Come here   I
I want you to do **SILLY** say, I want you
tricks, I want to

Doggy,

play! You bound towards me, I brace myself with glee, A fluffy wall crashes

into me. Head pats and scratches for the big ol' pupppy, If you   could

speak, You would scream happy happy happy! Doggy Doggy, Don't

ever leave me, I would miss you, Would you miss me? A kiss to   the

cheek, well, a lick so to speak, Yes Yes I would miss you a lot! Is probably

what he would say,   Who knows   at this point,
he is so silly   in different
little **Doggy** ways.

Mother

bird high in a nested

tree, Your children squawk

and squeak, You found them

abandon, Strewn about   in

separate trees, You   feed   them

literature, You tell them to never   abandon   thee,

Yet your children start to grow,   Knowledge absorbing

into their bones, Papers and words decorate their   premature

feathers. Soon they will leave the nest, Soon they will

be far from the rest. Your children won't all   be

in the same place, They will build their own

nests, They   will build it remembering your   grace,

Mother bird you shed a tear, The little ones will come back, So   don't

ou ever fear, Yet cry for now as the time draws near, Let your   wings

pan and nurture them, Until the day is here. You have fresh   flock,

Waiting for your call, You'll never forget us, Never at all. Mother,

ve will miss you, That's for sure, You didn't just help us fly,   Ms.

Oyche, Our precious mother bird, You helped us soar. We   will

MOTHER BIRD never forget   you

evermore

What are you to me? It's not   clear   you see, I didn't   even

Know, Not until my late   teens.   You're not related to   me,

So, what does that mean? Does   that make you friend? Or   does

that make you family? You're   not a stranger, You're not   a

cousin, Not even related   to   me, Yet you see I know who

you are to me, You're a sister   I   have receieved, No blood

Relates, But I'm as happy as can be,   Happy that you   and

me, Are related through a   brother   So, we're   basically

family! And that means the entire world to an only girl like me.

UNRELATED SISTER

THE END OF THE BEGINNING

I've done it,
but can I move on?
Can I leave everything behind?
Will anybody cry as I leave goodbye?
Who knows what the future holds,
Though I wish I could see,
See what the future has in store for me,
It's boring to know,
Everyone says wait and see,
And it'll come to me,
But I don't want to wait,
Because,
What if I don't succeed?
What if my heart bursts and bleeds?
Will I be able to do this?
Will I make people proud of me?
Oh well,
Let's see,
This only just the end,
The end of the beginning.

Mila Leeson is a poetry writer who dabbles in the intricacies of playful yet meaningful poetry. Having been introduced to a poetry editor position young in High School, Mila has taken to poetry and has learned from the writing of others on how to create poetry that draws the reader while also editing them and providing insight on said writings. Mila has been published a couple of times throughout grade school, one of them being Colgan High School's Literary journals, Siren and The Megalodon, which she has worked for since her junior year. Mila has also presented her work at open mic nights hosted by Colgan High School's Creative Writing program and other open mic nights local to the community. When she isn't writing, she's usually spending time with loved ones or thinking of new and unique ways to create her poems. There is still much more growth to occur, but still so much more to see if this book of poetry is considered for a good whimsical read.